SETTLING

SETTLING

POEMS BY

MARY LOGUE

MID-LIST PRESS
Minneapolis

Library of Congress Cataloging-in-Publication Data
Logue, Mary, 1952-
Settling : poems / by Mary Logue.
p. cm. ISBN 0-922811-33-4 (paper: alk. paper)
I. Title. PS3562.0456S4 1997
811'.54--dc21 97-34119 CIP

Manufactured in the United States

MID-LIST PRESS
4324 12th Avenue South
Minneapolis, Minnesota 55407-3218

Cover painting, "La Vallée," by Ilene Krug Mojsilov © 1996

Acknowledgments for previously published poems:
Minnesota Monthly: "A Comfort"
Minnesota State Arts Board newsletter: "Mid-Summer"
Minnesota River Review: "Wind"

The author thanks the Minnesota State Arts Board for its support.

For Peter
with love

Contents

Like a white stone in a deep well
one memory lies inside me.
  —Anna Akhmatova

I'm no more alone than usual
with this perfect history of snowing
so quietly without people.
  —James L. White

NINE SIMPLE POEMS IN WINTER

I

The taste of winter pear is soft and sweet.
Outside, the snow sinks in around the tall grasses.
The violet droops, not enough water, not enough light.

The hunters swarm through the hills,
searching for deer among the trees.
A gunshot echoes over the bluff.

The pear sits half-eaten, its whiteness exposed.
I hurt inside and instead of moving away
I'm going into it.

II

The sunlight is thin through a smear of clouds,
and on the lake there is an ice film—
the start of the long nights.

Wait for the day to end in light sorrow.
Wait for the night to crawl over the land.
The darkness is both a blanket and a cover.

When I wake at three, the hour of the wolf,
I'm alone again.
I hold my hand in front of my face to feel my breath.

III

The cafe was not crowded.
We drank wine, and you put your feet on the chair
next to me. I watched your eyes smile.

It was simple. The streets were empty.
In the bar you told me you liked my teeth.
They weren't perfect, you said.

The woman who was your wife
Is like a tree that cuts a shadow,
A slight shadow across your face.

IV

Three dead mice I found in a pail of water.
Their bodies were curled up, caught in the last stroke.
Carrying them by their tails, I laid them in the snow.

Overhead a bird flew up against the sky,
the wind burst beneath its wings.
The barn door banged open.

The cold was wet and raw
like a wound. The mice were apostrophes,
little moments that were gone.

V

The fire is dying, the embers
glow like the scraps of a sunset in
a deep black sky. They fade.

I think of sleeping, but turn to look at the sky.
Desires, like stars, prick me.
The heavens are full of glints of light.

To fight against the darkness
takes a strength that is only human—
a hand, some warmth, a touch.

VI

You ask me what I want.
The shade is drawn, but the light
seeps around the edges of the cloth.

I remember the tawny juice of peaches,
times when I wanted something so bad,
I could taste it.

Want is a word I need to learn again.
If I could answer you,
I'd be halfway down the road.

VII

The shed leans to one side.
Bare grape vines grab and hold it.
In the summer, swallows flew in its door.

Now the ice melts off the roof,
forming a river in the snow,
a path that no one follows.

The sun circles low in the sky.
The cherry trees won't blossom for months.
I wonder how long it will go on.

VIII

The fire dances on the hallway wall.
If I lift my head from my pillow, I can see it.
How good it is to watch something move and glow in the dark.

When I dream and fly in my sleep,
the earth is so close below me,
like a body I brush over.

No moon, no sounds, the night is gentle.
Slipping under the quilt, I remember
the silk of your skin pulling away from me.

IX

Frail light, yet it's enough
to see the food we are eating—
soup of beans and onions, dark bread.

Mist rose off the lake the morning
I went back to the city,
hinting at hidden water.

Long we talk into the night.
When you leave, something lifts from my eyes—
whatever will come, I feel, is already in the air.

—*Stockholm, Wisconsin*

SETTLING

for my father

The pond settles into late summer silt.
You sit close to the window day after day,
and watch sap pull from wood,
hum out of grass and sweet from flowers.
Petals fall, old silk from a plum
chrysanthemum. The low string of light
gets thinner on the horizon.
Clouded eyes fall to your knees.
You say a few words, then are quiet.
The garden is a darker place.

FORGETTING A LIFE

My father is forgetting his life.
In the living room he sits
on a throne of pillows,
near the wall of windows
overlooking the pond.

He can't remember his mother's
first name, won't remember
his father's offenses.
The aunts coming with éclairs
find the house empty;
my father has forgotten them.

He calls to ask
why we fired his caretaker.
I tell him she talked to
herself and threw him around.
"Oh," he says, "then all right."

He forgets what to say on the phone,
can't remember the days of the week.
He sleeps next to his radio,
a strain of Mozart a buzz in his ear
as he forgets where he is.

When the forgetting is done,
all there'll be to remember
is his death.

PHEASANT

There's no one left
to tell me how
to cook Grandma's pheasant.
Dad never knows these things.
All I have are thin memories
from when I was a kid.

Grandma Logue's been dead for twenty years.
We ate her pheasant in the fall
at a round table in her house in Waseca.
The house had no bathtub, only a gas heater.
Dad killed the bird the day before,
hunting in the fields around town.
Pheasant cooked for hours
in a black Dutch oven. Sweet meat
dripped into our mouths.

Maybe I wouldn't even like
the over-cooked fowl, but I remember
it caught something of my father
that I will never get enough of—
his walks through dying fields,
his aloneness—the only gifts
to his family
he knew how to give.

WRITING A WORD

My mother was a full, round woman
until a stroke cut her in half.
Right down the middle. With what precision
a pebble in the blood can roll.

No lilting landscape left in her voice,
her left hand hung like a dead pigeon
at her side, her left foot came along
for the ride, clomp, along for the ride.

Mom, how far is it to the other side
of your body?

I lean against the counter top and watch you
at the dining room table. Your feet dangle
from the chair. You're munching potato chips,
while your mind fumbles words that land

scrambled in the boxes of a crossword puzzle.
Nothing makes as much sense as it used to,
neither all your hopes nor all my fears.
I take your hand, and we write a word together.

WIND

Hanging sheets, I remember, my
Mother would hold the white cloth
to her nose and say to me, "Smell,
•the wind whips sunlight into them."

The sheets ripple and we pin them
to a line between two steel posts.
We're standing on the edge of a pond
and in it an angular egret is fishing

the shallows, picking into algae and muck.
Our hands are in clean wet t-shirts and socks.
When all the sheets are dry, we fold them
together between us and carry them into the house.

That all happened many years ago.
The egret flew away,
the sheets shredded,
but where is the wind? the women?

T E A

Could you come visit for afternoon tea?
I'd make it the way you like it, fresh water,

one heaping teaspoon of Nestea, a good stir in a tall glass,
ice, lemon. See the lemon slice, full and tart,

it waits for you. All I want is a short visit, a simple
conversation. Could you take

a moment to stop by?
I want to tell you of my life,

the dog that sits in sunlight like a cat,
the small farmhouse that snugs under the bluff,

the man who snores in bed and writes books, too.
I could show you my quilt, the budding Amaryllis,

the newly covered chair, the book I wrote about
your mother. The house on Deer Pond is going to be sold.

Dad is buried in a field of crosses next to you. Blankets
of snow cover the lakes. It's January

and I'm filling a tub with water for a late afternoon
bath. All creatures in the house are sleeping this Sunday

except me. I'm sitting at my desk, paying bills and
thinking I'd like to see you again, Mother,

one more time. I'd like to hear your voice telling me
that my life has the feel of a good heavy cloth

in your hands.

Memorial Day

I

Three days of shrouded sky.
Below it we open up the ground
and stick flowers in
a pattern which is pleasing
to the eye when seen from above.

Bending and rising, we finally worship
what we ought: the land, the rising warmth,
the spirit that runs in us like sap,
the energy that makes life fill out
the fans of a day lily.

II

Two crab apple trees
in such full bloom the eye wearies
of tracing the petals that lace the
fretwork of branches. Silent music
of soft pink petals. I try to
imagine a person suddenly budding
from every pore—such great beauty!
We would declare hosanna.

III

One year ago today
we gathered on the back lawn:
our family, three daughters and a tired
father. His body thinned to awkward grace,
hands floated to carry a cigarette to lips.
We all knew it would not happen again.
The dogs chased each other on the grass
and his eyes flew after them.

IV

No parents left, we plant flowers
and water trees, we lift an eye
to empty sky, a freighted gray,
we give the day away, a waft
of lilac scent, a handful of
petals lent, and remember
what a time we've had.

Mid-Summer

It's mid-summer and I dread the end
of it. Like losing a mother, soft hands
slipping into the earth. The wind has been
so full. Another breath.

These are the days when the light fades
a cock's stride earlier, a beat before
I'm ready, the sun blinks out and only
the glow of remembering tints the clouds pink.

Why is this moment of grace so close to sorrow?
Why can't I stay in it? Instead I feel the leaving,
a glove pulled off, a window shade pulled down,
pulled away, when I wanted a bit more.

A COMFORT

If I were given each day
as a piece of fabric:
the hue that permeated the sky,
the dusk off an apple, the fold of a hand,
you know, the stuff you gather.
If I had it as a square of cloth,
I could make a covering.
Nothing falls away,
we carry it all with us.
What funny rumply creatures we become.
I sit in the sunlight on the couch,
long winter afternoon slanting in on me.
I'm still except for my hands.
All the pieces are there
in my lap, what a life,
what a weight.
I keep sewing, the stitches
like words that hold the world together.
Give me another piece.
I know where it goes—
pain and hope sewn side by side
make a comfort.

WE THREE

There are two women in my life.
I, too, a woman, have no wife,
but these two closest like a whisper,
I call them both the same name, "sister."

One dark, one fair, they both
have hair like mine—curls in a froth.
Slight of weight, long of gait—
in ways, each other's mate.

Our mother's gone and father's dead.
We've sold the house, probate's read.
And now we ask what makes a family?
The rest are gone, it's just we three.

There's always blood to link us
but if you saw us you'd think us
three best friends, *des belles amies*.
For a good long while, there'll be we three.

DWINDLING ROSES

Dwindling roses lean against each other.
I walk with my younger sister.
The blue of the lake punches the sky:
Promises are so quickly broken.

I walk with my younger sister
who lives so far from me that
mountains grow and rivers flow
between us. Words are sparse.

Dwindling roses punch the sky,
soft bruise of early fall.
We open our eyes to the promises
no one can keep We lean against each other.

To be close to someone summons more
than the air and water roses
live on. I touch my sister's shoulder.
We are so quickly broken. But we walk.

UNKNOWN SORROW

I'll never know a mother's sorrow—
the green-lit marble of the *Pietà*
as she, so large, so powerful,
holds her grown child in her stone arms,
cradles him as if she could, once again,
give him life.

My own mother's sorrow
as her only son died one November night
(his long body sailed by rushing cars)—
her sadness went so deep
she would never climb out of it.
When my sister was murdered,
my mother turned toward her own death.
Years later, in early fall, as leaves tipped golden,
her heart broke the final time.

No longer able to bring a child
into the world, I often feel
easily unfettered. Yet I know
on the other side of that sorrow
is a joy I will never see,
a love that comes from
opening as wide as you can
and slipping someone else in.

FEAR OF FALLING

It is the movement to the edge
I fear, the coming around the corner,
the over the cliff, the emptiness,
the chasm chasing at me, that
I can't stand.

My body roils,
my heart flops inside me, my palms
bead sweat, my hands grip
tree, door handle, railing.
Solid is good.

I don't want to fall
into that deep canyon
where water moves like a green
snake and rocks hold
air prisoner, where people
have walked and then disappeared,
leaving not a sound, not a sign.

The abyss is a hiss of light,
a slit in the firm, the known.

SONNETS OF SENSE

I

The sky closes with clouds, opens with stars.
I too open and close, like a sea anemone.
The waves of an inner sea move me
or a force outside, the wind in the poplars.

And even when I try to understand, to make
a sense of what I see and feel, and how I move,
in the end I have to sink down and love
what and who I do with power and ache.

It isn't that I can't run away.
I remember my mother talking of working
in another state, wondering where she would stay.

While I appear to be here, while my body wanders
along, doing the dishes, washing
shirts and sheets, another part of me meanders.

II

Now that we live together, I know you more.
I've known you longer. I see you closer,
even though the house we live in is large. Behind a door
the faint clicking of keys; on the pillow a coarse hair

of yours. I hold it in my fingers and examine
the texture, the brownness of it.
When the phone rings, I lie still and listen
to your voice. This slip of hair is a bit,

a chunk of you. The conversation
we had last night hums in my ear.
It occurs to me to make a declaration

of how I feel. But love rings in silence.
I write this poem to say what I can,
knowing it serves only one sense.

III

For the blind the word is a series
of bumps. And I think that might be
true for me. A touch, a hollow, a hand to please
the landscape of the other's body.

At night we lose the enchantment
of the sighted world. Fall
into the rustling encampment
of the enemy. Black night is a wall.

There is the sound of cloth flapping,
the taste of honey made from clover,
the smell of musk, a river lapping

against our skin. And the lover
we've always wanted is there.
What if this dark night were never over?

IV

What sense is left when love enters?
Even far from you, over river and lake,
the thought of you centers
me, your voice leaves an ache.

It rained last night 'til after one,
then froze. Snow shone with ice glaze.
We had talked, I knew you couldn't come.
All day the air filled with ice haze.

It wasn't that I missed you, it was
that you weren't here
in this life of mist and rain. Does

that make sense? But there, I'm back again.
There is no sense to make of this.
Love's the center; around it we spin.

V

Touch me in the deep pit of my palm,
on my neck where my heart beats through.
I smell you and the sea grows calm,
I hear you and the sun slices through.

No sight is worth your shoulder.
The sand is wet where the sea hits.
Shiny mica clings to your lips, older
than anything, broken in bits

swirled up in the wind. I keep
wanting to make love a tangible,
a smellable, a thing, not this leap

of faith, not this crush
of feeling, unmanageable.
But I think too much. Touch.

FISHING

Waiting is really what it's all about.
The fish are there, below us in the water.
We know it, can feel them,
their thin envelopes of skin sliding through
dark water down so deep that I
spin out yards of line to reach them.

Hours move across the lake, pulling
shadows out of pine trees and laying
fingers of lights on the wave tips.

Talk is slow and lazy as we drift.
Nothing serious, that's the rule,
because your mind has to be on
what you're doing when you're fishing.
You have to want to catch a fish,
you tell me. I dangle a foot
over the edge of the canoe and
you drink a lukewarm beer.

We never catch anything, and later I think
about all I actually wanted: the long afternoon,
your voice a breeze in my ears, the knowledge
of another life going on below me
in that liquid silence, seeing my line as a
possibility and then swimming away.

NIGHT MOVEMENT

for Peter

The rippled glass of the window pane holds
a bowl of early apples and a candle stuck in a beer bottle.

Beyond are the cut-outs of birch and pine trees,
boathouse on the shore of Burntside Lake,

water like faded blue jeans, opposite shore
the darkest band of black and then the sky

leaving as I write, the sun gone, the afterglow
slipping away. Tonight there'll be silence and stars.

We'll slip, we'll fade into sleep, yet even
in the core of night, the furthest from light,

even in the deepest of the going away, the leaving,
I'll feel you next to me and know it's time to start to come back.

To Marry

for Dodie and David

Standing quietly next to a brimming
meadow we might hear a bird
that we've never heard before
sing a few notes. The notes,
in their purity, float in the air
long after the bird has flown away.

When we humans try to
sing, to raise our voices and praise
what we see around us, tell of the people
that fill our lives like black-eyed Susans
dappling a meadow,
we call it loving.
A simple act where we step
beyond the surface of our skin
and hear another's heartbeat.

Let us all marry today.
Let us toast our mothers and fathers
who married before us.
Let's drink the dark wine of the earth
and the light wine of the sky.
To marry is to praise another,
to sing a note that lasts a lifetime.

LASTING LOVE

The nudge of a shoulder at night,
that's love, or flash of first light
on a cream wall. Not the ground under us,
not the ocean embracing the land with blue.
Bits of brightness, bites of richness,
kiss, wave, touch, blink.
It's there, it's gone. I'll never
hold it, pin it to my chest.
I turn. You're down the hall.
There's only a few air-filled feet between us.
It lasts that long.

SIMPLE LOVE

for Robin and Paul

I can find no happy love poems.
Can it be that while we love
we only think of loss?
Or that love overwhelms us
like a wave in an ocean
we can never cross?

Let's make it simple.
You see that flower in the window.
It blooms because of the light,
and the water
that has rained down on it,
and the good dark earth
anchoring its roots.

Can we look at a man
or a woman and not think of
how love has transformed them?
The air opens before them
and they move more easily.

The sadness, it probably comes from thinking.
When one simply feels love,
the flower blooms, that's it.
The white flower bursts open and blooms.

CONSTANT

I hear you in the next room,
your fingers on the keyboard,
your feet walking over the carpet;
a slight whistle indicates
a thought has landed, been captured,
set free. You are in my life
so deeply that I turn around you.
I am in shadow, then light.
I am near you, then away.
All is measured by this distance.
When I first met you I knew how
the ancients felt being told
the flat world was round.
I saw circles on your shoulders
as you held me in the dark.
I know we won't be together
forever; the love I get from you
is more constant than that.
This feeling is not held
within time. It is, rather, air.
Even when we do not breath it,
the space it fills is alive.

RASPBERRIES

Such sweetness in a tiny red bowl,
built around a pip of white.
The blue sky has a drift of clouds.
I'm in a field of raspberries and
pearly everlastings—furry white flowers
with deep yellow centers. The bees are
bumbling from flower to flower and I'm
ambling from bush to bush. There's a
hum from wings, and whirs. I lift up
a leaf and see the jewel drops of red
but only take the berries
that fall off into my hand.

PERFECT

I want it to stay perfect:
purple phlox unfurled to its fullest,
nasturtium blossoms afloat on a bed of green leaves,
hollyhocks straight against the white wall,
blossoms opening at the bottom.

And one weekend in late July,
all is at its prime
like a picture.
I was there.

Snap, they fade, they fold.
Snap, we bend and break.
And in this imperfection
I see the seeds of a new flower.

How to Do T'ai Chi

Don't wait for the right time.
Rather, do it when you're too busy.
When work, dishes, and lover
lean on you like the side of a mountain,
push into mountain.
Hold it in your belly, your *tan tien*,
grind it up and pave the land
for the step of your foot
as it comes down with
the lightness of the first snow,
the comfort of a hand on shoulder,
the force of that old mountain again.
It doesn't go away, that mountain.
We go to it, we move back.
We wave our hands like clouds,
we fling our manes like horses.
We stand on one leg to spin
and the world turns.
The last few steps
the earth rises up to meet us.

THE BEAUTY OF OLD BODIES

In the locker room, old women bend
and take off their clothes.
I watch them.
On the border of their country,
I want to see
what will happen to me.
The folds of their bodies
tend toward earth.
These aging women move
as if they have more time than I do;
they carefully hang their clothes up
and wrap towels over their breasts.

I lie in the sauna with them
and see their bodies as pots
that hold more
than is comfortable.
They're dimpled
and rumpled with life,
curving and sagging
with the stuffing that flavors it.
Their flesh is soft and in dim light
doesn't look like marble,
but flows
like a worn cloth
generous in its cut.

I trembled at the first puckering
of my skin
and I'm sure I'll wince again,
but in a heated glow,
I see that beauty
comes from enduring life,
carrying it within.

GARBAGE

All week long we drop pieces into this plastic bag:
browning apple cores, unread letters, crumbs

from the edges of plates. On Thursday,
I push down the pile and tie a knot.

With the bag on my hip, I open the back door.
Night hums in the shabby leaves of the maple.

The moon flutters above the garage.
As I walk, the bag grows smaller and lighter.

My worries are white paper, disposable.
Darkness has its own smell.

THE NEST

In me there rests a poem just as in the thinning maple tree,
leaves falling like so many years dropping away, there sits on a dark

branch a nest woven of gathered bits: twigs and grass and threads. And this
poem is about the search for home, the years dropping away,

the yellow leaves growing more beautiful as they age.
This poem is about opening a door and you smiling at me

for a moment and then stepping into my life. The nest will be left
in the tree this winter after the leaves have fallen away.

SUMMER NIGHTS

In the long nights of summer the town sighs.
On Spring Street, known also as "J," a single car

is parked on it in front of the hotel. A splurt of water
runs out from under the stores, hidden springs feeding

into a sluice that goes down to the lake. To say
it's quiet neglects the lick of electricity

in the Short Stop sign, the burl-burl of crickets
rubbing and jouncing, the drawn-out howl of the freight

trains slipping down from the Twin Cities to Chicago.
I order a Leiney's for the road; the barkeep opens

the bottle for me and hands it back with a wink. Blessed,
I head home; above me the Covenant church cross

beams down, bright bulbs attracting veiled, flitting moths—
like obsessive thoughts they fly in circles. Through the windows

of my house a hanging light shines and I walk toward it,
thinking of sleep as an answer to a question that

never gets asked.

PERSPECTIVE

Below us the land sifts to black.
A river pulls through this darkness like a silver thread.
The sun is a red yolk,
and the sunset, half a sky wide.

We are soaring in an empty heaven.

These moments above the earth
show it to be a place we barely know,
wide and rolling, comfortable in its grandeur.

Having flown out of my life for a month,
I now see its infinite smallness:
phone calls, student papers, grocery lists,
and, once in a while, a good cry in the bathtub.

The earth is larger than I know,
my life is smaller than I thought.
This is called perspective—
what we do with the world.

Make the river a vein on a woman's leg,
gray clouds just filmy curtains
to be pulled across a window.
And the sun, a yoke, when we
want to hold it in our hands.

Desert Aubade

Through thin curtains light enters.
Your back, turned toward me, mounds like sand.

I know if I get up the day will start:
the quail pecking and bobbing at the feed on the patio,

early morning rain pulling scent from *piñon*
while *palo verde* glisten a softer green.

There are many ways to keep a moment;
one is to not step into it too soon.

Believing

If there is one atom in us
that continues, a thought
carried on, a moment
lived again, isn't that enough
to believe in?

BED

On entering
the bed does not seem irresistible,
but on the point of departure
it is the only place I want to be—
a cave of covers.

Sleep flutters in my eyes
like a curtain in the breeze.
All is possible,
all in front of me,
but I'd like to rest
a few more minutes.

DISTANCE

I'm standing in a phone booth
next to a bridge over the Corrib River.
Swans float by, their black feet moving them
so subtly it seems it is the river that causes
them to wander. Ducks light on the water.
You answer the phone on the third ring—

six hours and thousands of miles away
in the middle of our country. I've pulled you
out of sleep—an even further land—and you
don't want to leave it. *The trip is fine,*
I say. *We've had three flat tires. Punctures,*
they call them. One going into Dublin, and I had
to haul a tree into the road to protect

us from traffic. You tell me of work,
of meetings, of mutual friends. But you are
distant. There is no touch in the air
between us. I can't seem to get to you.
I know where I am.
I'm among pools of rain water left from a storm,
in a country of bending and culling swans,
but I've no idea where you've gone.

ALIVE IN NEW BUFFALO

The beach at New Buffalo, Michigan,
is covered with sand, fingers of driftwood,
and plastic bread bags—for picnics,
I suppose. The sand is a fine dusky gray
that sticks to your toes.
This afternoon I almost died on the freeway
when a state trooper stopped in the slow lane
and a trucker pulled into the middle lane
where I sat in my pristine little red Isuzu,
not a mark on it in two years, 43
miles to the gallon, and I was singing along
to the O'Kanes when the trucker's left fender
touched, then pushed the right side of my car and
tore up my wheel and bounced my head
around, and instead of braking I pulled away
and watched in my rearview mirror as
the truck slid across all lanes, jack-knifing, then
twisting, the cabin roof coming down
to touch the driver. I pulled off to the side
of the road, watching him climb out of the
driver's door window up to the sky.
Out of my car, I leaned on the guard rail,
saying simply to myself over and over again,
like a mother crooning, "I'm alive, I'm alive."

I'm eating lobster and watching as
an old woman walks by, her stomach protruding
more than her old breasts, but she is
full of vigor. She has sap in her arms and
legs and she is moving quickly toward the beach.
I've eaten lobster so infrequently
that I don't even know how to
but I pull it apart and tear and suck.
Rich, red flesh. After dinner I go
to the beach and remember the truck driver
took one look at his pizza truck loaded with cheese
and knew he had lost his job. "But I didn't
kill anyone." This is the line he says
to pull himself up. I walk
down to the water and stand watching the
lake turn dark as tarnished silver. I see
the old woman swimming in the dusk, and I
decide to grow old, to become her,
to swim in life until the light
fades away and the water drops off
the edge of the earth.

Not Sopadilla

I try to learn their names,
bougainvillaea, sopadilla, magnolia,
but this tree I don't know:
frilly fragrant petals, thin orchid-like flower
peppered through tree branches, long
seed pods hanging down. On the way
to the bakery, I stop and ask
an old woman who has two of these
trees in her yard, what they are.
She doesn't hear me. I get off
my bike. She turns, laughs about
her bad hearing, and comes toward me,
tottering, white frizzy hair a tent on her head,
dress coat a sack on her body,
in her arms a foggy-eyed Chihuahua.
What are these trees? I ask.
These two, she says, pointing,
there's one with white flowers,
the other purple. I don't know.
I don't remember the name, but
all you need to grow your own
is a seed. The dog lunges at me.
She shoves him back with a quick slap.
Come any time and take a seed pod.
Make sure it's purple and dry.

Come, she pats my arm. The flowers,
unnamed, are no less fragrant. *Come
and take the seeds.* I never learn
the name of the tree, but the light
touch of her hand on my arm,
the urging to take a seed, I will
always know.

STORM

Bats rumbled in the walls,
thunder flew across the sky,
the storm pulled a pane off a window
and I woke at the sounds,
wondering where I was.
Would no one hold me?
The sleep I found later
was remote and insubstantial
like an island in a far northern lake.

An Invitation

There is a place not far from here:
a farmhouse sheltered by bluffs, with
outbuildings leaning softly like old stones.

In the house is a room filled with dusk,
light you can slip your hand through.
In the room is a bed, sheets stretched taut,

pillows for two heads. This place is not far.
The road to it is winding and lined with trees,
valleys deep with hushed grass. Come visit.

SNOWING

One winter it never quit snowing. The sky would breathe
in for a day or two, then out and snow would fall.

A finely tatted lace hung in the branches of the maple,
covered the compost pile, the unraked leaves. Like

insignificant memory, it kept falling until there was no
darkness left. What power knows that in the dead of winter

trees and hills should be put to rest, a shroud of forgetfulness
thrown like bits of paper, empty of words, filled with peace?

WINTER STORM

Sky scoured with snow, the light left
glimmers through, the lake heft
of snow and ice dazzles. A storm
has blown the warmth away, left form.

If I prayed it would not be to god,
even the name offers a limit to laud.
Yet in this winterness I praise the snow,
I watch the wind, I know its blow.

Can there be such a place, such a time
such a landscape without rhyme,
sky of a like color without a hand
behind it all, pushing the wind off the land?

But not to know is what it is
that I believe in. There is no His.
The stippled snow, the frosted fall,
the weathered wind, I praise it all.

FALLING SNOW

Ice is growing on the windowpanes.
—Anna Akhmatova

Here, in this world of deaths, I do nothing
but sit on the couch and watch the snow fall.
Beside me lies the dog, a black puddle.

Night is even blacker, and beyond that
an emptiness I can only guess at.
I know a lake churns, far out in the darkness,
coated with slab ice three feet deep.

Alone, I sit quietly and reach
my toes to touch the warm floor, breathe
in a deep gulp of air and take comfort
in all I know. I watch the snow float down.

For a moment and a swirl, it may fly upward,
but after, the snow continues to fall to earth. It settles.
There is no throwing it back in the sky.

So my mother and father and sister and brother
will remain dead the rest of my life.
I walk without them. I eat at a table
with too many chairs. I hold on to missing them.

The snow swarms the lights like bees around honey.
Summer will come and grass will push up under
the white glove of all this snow. The dead
will always stay on the other side of the glass.

HOUSE BLESSING

Bless this house
that holds within
fire and water
talk and listen
ceiling and floor
creature and man.

Bless this house
that holds without
lightning and dust
tree branch and flower
road and stone
man and creature.

Bless this house
without and within.
We make it home.

DONE

Done dishes
dried leaves
soft hands
simple things
salt shaker
shingled roof
slippered feet
sleeping cat
cupped hands
come home.